W9-AOT-840

LIFE
in
HAREM

K.ERHAN BOZKURT

Written by	: K. Erhan Bozkurt
Translation	: Aylin Alkoç
Photos by	: Selamet Taşkın, Keskin Color Archive
Graphics by	: Mehmet Süha Coşar
Type Set	: Deniz Çıra
Colour Separation	: Renk Grafik
Published and Printed	: Keskin Color Kartpostalcılık Ltd. Şti. Matbaası
Distributed	: Keskin Color Kartpostalcılık San. ve Paz. A.Ş. Ankara Cad. No. 98 34410 Sirkeci - İSTANBUL Tel.: 0 (212) 514 17 47 - 514 17 48 - 514 17 49 Fax: 512 09 64
Branch Office	: Kışla Mah. 54. Sk. Günaydın Apt. No. 6/B 07040 ANTALYA Tel.: 0 (242) 247 15 41 - 247 16 11 Fax: 247 16 11

ISBN 975-7559-87-3

1998
© copyright by KESKİN COLOR AŞ

CONTENTS

4

Dear Readers,

This book has been primarily prepared for visitors who come to travel around in and learn about Turkey, and who are interested in Ottoman history. Harem has always been a subject not much delved into, and embellished with exaggerated hearsay and imaginary information not only for foreigners but also for Turkish people, because in-depth researches, as well as being scarce, have only started to be brought out to daylight within the last decades. Moreover, since Harem was the place where the secret private lives of Ottoman dynasty is spent, no kind of information could be expected to leak out of here. This scarcity of information has unfortunately provided an opportunity for the creative dreams of native and foreign writers to flourish.

This book is the first one to deal with harem in its entirety for foreigners who have come to our country. No information in the book is in any way designed in an attractive or exaggerated manner so as to please its readers an gain their interest. Its intention is to narrate the realities of its day as they were to the today's people, because we believe that absolute realities can any way be so interesting as to fascinate people. The important thing is to find and reveal them.

All of the information found in the book depends upon the results of the researches that competent native historians made in the Ottoman archives. After having dwelved upon several points we found important about harem, we included a small guide appendix that gives explanations useful along the walk path of harem. We hope that the explanations of some words that we prepared for the end of the book will be helpful for the readers.

K. Erhan Bozkurt
İstanbul 1997

THE WORD "HAREM"

The word "harem" originates from Arabic and means "the thing or person that is forbidden." The places called harem are either totally forbidden to enter or can be entered under the constraints of some prerequisites. For instance, for centuries Mekke and Medine have been the forbidden cities, where non-muslims could not enter and they were called "Haremeyn", meaning "the place that is forbidden." But the word "harem" does not only indicate a spatial prohibition but also a sexual one, because "harem" is also used in meaning of the women of a muslim man. It is in the sense that these women are forbidden to any men except for their husbands. Unmarried women are "free" for their prospective husbands, but married women are "haram". Harem is the noun form of "haram," i.e. that is forbidden. Just as the women of muslim men, the women of sultans were called "harem". This institution was called "Perde" or "Zenane" in India, "Enderun" in Iran and "Harem" in the countries under the influence of Arabic culture. Ottomans used to call this part of the palace "Der'üssaade", i.e. "house of bliss", but its characteristic of being forbidden has come so much to the foreground that, people outside found it appropriate to call it, as it is today, "Harem".

POLYGAMY

The social roots of polygamy lies undoubtedly hidden deep in the history of mankind, ever since the patriarchal societies have come into being. Within the context of our subject, we are only concerned with how Islam, views polygamy, which we'll mention briefly. Islam, through its holy book, Koran, wanted to establish an order to prevent polygamy from being abused in an immoral manner. With this intention, in those years when barbarous features weren't totally absent from societies. Islam permitted men who were economically sufficient to marry up to four women. In order not to be unjust towards women, the responsibilities of men towards women are explicitly explained in Koran. However, these rules have no legal efficacy in today's Turkey. In Turkey, marriages are established in Register Office of Marriages and can be broken only by court. The regulation of marriage is actualized by Civic Law.

For instance, Islamic Law, that is practiced in Iran and Saudi Arabia, has no efficacy in Turkey, but minority of the population - usually the members of a sect - try to maintain their lives according to Islamic rules, still eventually they have to obey the Civic Law of Turkish Republic. Since the times of **Atatürk**, polygamy has been abolished and at the same time forbidden. However, still we find some man, in our country, who are "married" to more than one woman despite this prohibition. These men are legally married to only one woman, and they can only make a religious marriage, which does not have any efficacy before the laws with the other women, and this cannot go any further than being a private contract made between two people. Under these circumstances, only if one the government begin a legal procedure.

ATATÜRK: Founder of modern Turkey

HISTORY OF HAREM

Ottomans, as all sovereigns, depended on the growing of new generations to maintain their existence. During the Foundation Era of the Ottoman Empire in the fourteenth century, sovereigns and the princes would marry especially the daughters of governors who were Turk, East Roman, Bulgarian or Serb in origin or of elite families. These intertribal marriages naturally had to be done within the framework of a policy based on interest. Osman Bey, the founder of the Ottoman Empire and the first Turkish sovereign who adopted an extension policy, was himself married to two noble women Turkish in origin. However, his son, Orhan Bey was married to four women, three of whom were foreign and one of whom were Turkish in origin. Geographic conquerism due to economic and political reasons, began with Osman Bey, intertribal marriages began with his son Orhan Bey. The first six sovereigns Ottoman Empire were married to at least two (Prince Osman and Mehmet Çelebi) and at most five women (Orhan Bey, Murad I, Yıldırım Bayezit and Murad II). These women belonged to noble families, but only the two wives of Osman Bey were Turkish and muslim in origin, the wives of other sovereigns were mostly daughters of the royal families of the countries mentioned above. With these marriages, Ottomans were maintaining an intelligent policy based on balance between kingdoms. By the help of these marriages, they were forming temporary and tactical unions with both Turkish tribes-yet independent then and with the royal families or strong and opposing families in Balkan region and of Eastern Roman Empire. For instance, after becoming emperor, Kontakuzesus VI, in return for the help he got from Orhan Bey, as a sign of gratitude and friendship, he made his daughter Theodora, from his

Sultan Mehmed II

wife Irene, marry Orhan Bey. The wedding was held in the May of 1346 and Şehzade Halil Bey was the offspring of this marriage. This kind of "purposeful" intertribal marriages continued to be made until the end of the reign of Sultan Mehmed II (1451 - 81), the conqueror of Istanbul. With his reign, state underwent a process of rearrangement. Military affairs, the institution of Civil Service and finally the comprehension of "Harem" were rearranged within the framework of a definite state policy. "Harem" too, with which we will deal in our book and which plays a determinative role for centuries in the political life as well as in the life of the palace, has been formed in this era of the empire and has formed its

structure which will last for centuries and will be remmebered with imaginary fairytales and narratives. With Sultan Mehmed the Conqueror, Ottomans reached their most important political and economical aims: Constantinople. The most important commercial center in Little Asia was now under their hegemony and having destroyed Eastern Roman Empire totally in the may of 1453, they declared themselves to be the only power in Little Asia. It was not any longer necessary for the empire to establish relationships between kingdoms foreign to itself through marriages with foreign noble women as it was during the Foundation Era. In the Balkans, in Anatolia and in Arab Peninsula, there was not

7

remaining a more powerful state than the Ottomans. Now they were so powerful as to dictate under which conditions they wanted to live with their neighbours and with their economical and political rivals. Ottomans also had no intention of sharing the hegemony they established and the land they governed with neither Turkish-muslim tribes which could be rivals to them nor with the Christian kingdoms or powerful families that live in the Balkans. Consequently "Enderun-i Hümayun" (recruition school) was founded and only the children of non-Turk and non-muslim families, between 14 and 18 years of age were accepted. These were educated as the Ottomans' most striking power, janisaries, and as officers and ministers for the high degrees of government; Viziers (= Ministers), War Ministers, architects, etc.

Last Sadrazam (Grand Vizier) of Turkish origin, Vezir Çandarlı Halil Paşa, who was killed by Sultan Mehmed the Conqueror, was from Çandarlı family of Turkoman clans, which had a power enough to be a rival of Ottoman dynasty. In this way, a probable rival was eliminated. In order to prevent new and potential rivals from coming to important government posts, children, who were not from Turkish-Muslim families but who were from the minorities that lived within the borders of the empire and would not constitute danger, were educated as governors. With this intention, primarily the children of Albanian, Greek, Bulgarian, Serb, Armenian, Bosnian and Hungarian families were taken and educated. Thus, Sultan Mehmed the Conqueror was averting struggles about the throne that could even cause civil war, because those recruited (collected from subject minorities) statesmen had power only in the palace, but in the society they did not have masses that they colud drag behind them so as to emerge as a rival to Ottomans. In short, recruited ones were the most loyal servants for the Ottomans.

Another way of avoiding powers that could be rivals was keeping away from establishing relationships by way of marriage with Turkish tribes or foreign kingdoms by not marrying their daughters. In short, marriages intertribal that was unavoidable for Ottomans to exist and develop during the Foundation Era, were not considered to be appropriate after the empire was strengthened, but were seen as a concept to be refrained from. Because Eastern Roman Empire and some Turkish clans have disappeared as the consequence of this intelligent marriage policy of Ottoman, in order to protect itself from the irreparable consequences of such relationships, "harem" has structured according to this aim. As a result, Ottomans did not want to be the victim of a "weapon" that with consistent policies made them become superior to other societies. We would like to emphasize, in paranthesis, that the foundation and development of Ottomans were definitely eased by convenient economic conditions. However, as these facts, are not within the scope of our subject we will not go into that. We have brought the marriage policy of the Ottomans to the foreground intentionally as it is, with respect to our subject, closer to us. The intertribal marriage policy that Ottomans maintained emerged as the logical consequence of its endeavour to exist, being a small vanguard Turkish tribe that was situated on the farthest Western end and that is the lone border neighbour to Eastern Rome, but in the new approach which occurred after the conquest of Istanbul, "harem" that was institutionalized was the redesigned and reconstructed form of the marriage policy. This was nothing more than a new expression of the will of Ottoman dynasty to maintain its existence.

THE STRUCTURE OF HAREM

Harem in Topkapı was constructed approximately 70 years after the palace was built. In the earlier years harem was in the old and first palace building which was on the third hill of Istanbul at Beyazit where now Istanbul University is situated. While sultan was spending his family life at this old palace, he was executing the business of state from Topkapı Palace, which can be called as the bureaucratic center. Sultan Süleyman the Magnificent started the consruction of harem upon the insistence of his wife Roxalane, because she wanted to live at Topkapı Palace, where she could directly be in the political life. During the reign of Murad III (1574 - 95) the sections that stand up were formed. This places that provided a secure environment for the Ottomans for about 380 years, were left during the reign of Sultan Abdülmecid (1839 - 61), after Dolmabahçe Palace (1853), which has a more splendid and modern design, that can still succeed in fascinatign people at our day at the side of Bosphorus, was built. Harem, with which we are acquainted from written and official sources, and which is dealt with before we did in the publications of foreign countries and which is embellished with a striking and imaginary perception, is the one

Sultan Abdül Aziz

Three Ladies from Harem

in Topkapı Palace. Most of the events that are found in our book Life in Harem are those that happened in this Harem.

An institution like "Harem", which had a very important function, had to be arranged well and protected strictly. Indeed, when we examine we are faced with a very rationally designed complex of buildings that was taken under strict protection. First of all, we should think of this building as the house of sultan, where he spent his private life with his family. In this house, sultan him-self, his mother - the most powerful woman of the empire -, his wives and his children from them, women especially chosen and "cariye"s (female slave) lived. In this complex of buildings, as well as living areas, there were classrooms for the children of the sultan and the servants. Except these, in harem, which consisted of 400 rooms, there were Turkish baths, prayer rooms, libraries,

toilets, sitting rooms, courtyards, bedrooms, kitchen and a hospital. The apartments of the members of the dynasty and servants were naturally separate. Except for the members of the dynasty, approximatly 400 or 500 people lived in harem. These were the personnel that served in return for a certain wage. During the reign of Sultan Murad III (1574-85) 500, during the reign of Sultan Mahmud II (1809-39) 298 and during the reign of Abdülaziz (1861-76) 809 servant cariye s worked. However the people of harem were not so crowded since its formation in 16th. century until the 17th. century, because until the 17th. century, the mothers of the princes used to live with their other children and servants in the region where their sons ruled as the governor. After the 17th. century heirs to the throne began to stay at Topkapı Palace and lead a kind of prisoner's life. At this time new sections for heirs

were added to harem, therefore the need for servants naturally increased and during the 19th. century, the number of servants increased up to 809. A very good organization had to be done to direct such a crowded group of servants in line with an aim. Therefore a labour division based on ability and appearance was carried out among the maids in the groups depending on authority and hierarchical relations.

All of the men and women personnel in harem were in the status of slaves, but when we look at the places especially spared for them to live in, we see that they were not leading an inhuman life devoid of all rights as in other countries. The toilets, prayer rooms, and chambers spared for them in harem were properly kept appropriate for a living and clean. Slave trade was banned first in Istanbul in 1847, and then within the entire borders of the empire in 1857 by the Ottomans.

View of the Harem complex

Detail from the Sultan salon

Roof of Pergola in the Sultans salon

MALE PERSONNEL: THE EUNUCHS

It is possible to see that the traces of castration go back to antiquity. The first places eunuchs (a castrated man in charge of an Oriental harem and a high officer in the Palace) were used for service were Asur Palaces in Mesopotamia and this dates back to 2 thousand years earlier than today. From there it spread to Iran, India and China. Furthermore, the use of eunuchs in service is also observed in the West, as it passed from over Anatolia to Greeks and from there to Italians. For instance, one of seven the wonders of the world, colossal Temple of Artemis in Ephesus was protected by eunuchs.

The male personnel that served in harem would be castrated and were called eunuchs. Until the year of 1584, these were chosen from among the white war slaves of Slav, German or Hungarian origin. It was also possible to come across those of Armenian, Georgian or Circassian origin. These slaves, called "Ak Aga" (= White Master) in official records, were bought from the merchants already castrated, and only on exceptional occasions were they castrated in the Palace.

Merchants were castrating the young boys either by cutting off some part of their sexual organs or by wringing their testicles until they lost their function. If the manly feeligns of a eunuch were still aroused, they would be immediately suspended from their jobs. Sultan would pay them "azadlık" (indemnity of freedom) to make them pass from slavery to free life and establish a life for themselves.

A witness who lived in 1610s and worked with eunuchs in the palace told his observations as: "I witness that the betrayal of these negro infidels is such that, each of them falls in love with one or two female slaves (= cariye) and spends all of what they earn on them, sees and makes love to them whenever he finds the opportunity, and if it is said that they are castrated and they have no passion, man without passion cannot fall in love and feel compassion for women. Furthermore, these infidels keep on fighting with each other for women." As it is obvious in this narrative, the eunuchs had not always been devoid of sexuality. During the reign of Sultan Mahmud II (1808 - 39) three white eunuchs, each being paid 50 Kuruş (piastres), were dismissed from harem because of this reason.

Although in foreign publications they mention hundreds of castrated slaves, in the sources of the palace we see that only about a hundred eunuchs worked at the same time. For instance, it is recorded that during the reign of Sultan Mehmet the Conqueror 20 eunuchs, in 1517 40 castrated slaves worked in the palace. These eunuchs would keep guard at "Medhal" (the entrance section of Harem) and could not certainly enter Harem. They would also do the minor works of the people of Harem. For example, they would bring the meal they took from the kitchen outside to the main entrance of harem, leave it on the bank specially designed for that purpose and retreat. Female servants would come next, take in the meal and serve. Another duty of chief eunuchs was to lock all the gates at night and open again early in the morning.

The eunuchs would accompany the women of harem in their trips outside. Still it was certainly forbidden for them to look in the eyes of the women and they were obliged to look down when they saw a face without veil.

Chief Eunuch

Music making Harem lady

KIZLAR AĞASI (MASTER OF GIRLS, HEAD OF HAREM)

The head of Harem lived at the entrance of harem with the eunuchs. Although he himself was castrated, his rank was the highest among the male and female servants. His post came right after that of Viziers and Seyhülislam (the highest rank representative of Islam within the borders of the empire). He had a very influential position in the political life. There were a few positions held for a long time by the same person, and one of them was that of the head of Harem, because this post was given to people in whom Sultan could feel great confidence. For instance Eunuch Besir Aga carried on this duty for 30 years, Mehmet Aga of Abyssinian (Ethiopian) origin for 17 years and Yusuf Aga for 16 year. After the duration of their duty came to an end, they usually went to living in Egypt, sometimes in Cyprus, but always within the borders of the empire.

In 1582, Sultan Murad III, by dismissing White Eunuchs from their jobs and making Castrated Mehmed Ağa, a negro of Abyssinian origin, the head of Harem, made one of the most important positions of the palace to be held by negro eunuchs until the fall of the empire. Their influence had so much increased that they played an important role in some of the intrigues schemed to dethrone sultans.

The head of Harem was the senior of all of the male and female personnel in harem. He performed his job by using eunuchs under his command. Among his principle duties were providing the protection of harem and of the wives of Sultan, buying new female slaves, informing sultan about the promotion or punisment of the personnel and dealing with the arrangements of various ceremonies and entertainment.

A Harem Lady

FEMALE PERSONNEL: CARIYES

The most of the people of harem were "cariye"s (female slaves). All of the women in harem were in the status of slaves and Sultan would sleep with those who were especially chosen among them without getting married. Because of the preservations we mentioned earlier, Sultans were unwilling to marry free and noble women. The marriage of Sultan Osman II with the daughter of Şeyhülislam (the highest rank representative of Islam within the borders of the empire), Akile Hanım, in 1621 was an exception, but the fact that neither of the two sons of the sultan, the offspring of this marriage became Sultan is not a coincidence, because if one of the sons of Akile Hanım had come to the throne, she would have become Sultan's mother, the most powerful woman of the empire, and could have come to a position to make her relatives gain power. However, Sultan Osman II was killed at the age of 18, after a reign of four years, and his step brother Sultan Murad IV ascended to the throne instead. In order to avoid this threat Sultan Mehmet the Conqueror structured harem and solved the problem in a peaceful manner.

We can group the servants whose number could mount up to 800 in three categories: women who are merely servants, girls who are liked and especially chosen to be with by sultan and the wives of sultan. Although there were differences with respect to their functions and duties, they had one thing in common: Being a "cariye". They were all slaves, and only the sultan or his mother could grant them their freedom. This situation is explicit in the letters that the

Ewer Team at work

Harem Ladies at an entertainment in winter

wives of sultans wrote. Almost all of these letters written to sultan were signed as "Your cariye...". For instance, Roxelane (Hürrem Sultan), whose fame transcended the borders of the empire and who played an effective role in the political life of the era, signed her letters with this name. As it is obvious, whatever the status of the women were, a servant or a favourite or the wife of the sultan, being a "cariye" was not something pejorative. Even their living or working in harem provided them privilege within the borders of the empire. Furthermore, if they managed to become the especially chosen women or the wife of Sultan, they would have a more privileged place in harem and they would have been taken under protection on social terms. Cariyes could get their freedom before their jobs came to an end when they wanted to get married. In such a case, cariye would inform Sultan or his mother first with the

mediation of her "master" (senior) and then Head of Harem. The sultan would immediately have her dowry and the amount of money required to be given prepared. This kind of leaving the post was called "çırağ etmek."

It was the tradition that Sultans would make high officers marry the girls in his harem, among these were the women that he had earlier chosen especially and no longer liked or women that he wanted to dismiss because they caused discord in harem. Thus, these girls could find the opportunity to live a life close to palace although they left harem, and officers could be married with women who received education in the palace and knew the life in palace well.

Sultans would make the statesmen of the highest office marry Sultanas, i.e. his daughters or sisters. These statesmen were generally Viziers, Admirals, Ministers of Internal Affairs and Pashas of highest rank.

Thus these recruited statesmen of non-muslim origin were made a member of the dynasty. Generally the sultan himself would decide which sultana would marry which officer. The prospective son-in-law would be informed about the decision of the sultan in a written form by Vizier and he would be ordered to send his engagement presents to harem as soon as possible. Upon this order, the prospective son-in-law would immediately divorce his present harem, a prerequisite to be able to marry a sultana of the dynasty. Son-in-law was also made to owe a high amount of money to Sultan. If he wanted to divorce the sultana, he was to pay for this debt first. This debt, called "Mihr-i Müeccel" (postponed debt), could worth between 10 thousand and 300 thousand Kuruş (piastres) or gold, but if sultana herself or Sultan wanted the divorce, it would immediately be executed.

SERVANTS

The servants in harem were the personnel responsible from daily household duties:

a) Acemiler (= novices), were still being trained and did not have any administrative responsibilities.

b) Cariyeler (= slaves, maids), would carry out the simplest housework like cleaning, washing up under the supervision of a master or stewardess.

c) Kalfalar (= Stewardess), were more experienced and would perform their duties either by themselves or by the help of Cariyes.

d) Ustalar (= masters, experienced slaves), had done the longest service in Harem and were considered to be the heads of the teams. They would organize the division of labour and get the orders directly from the **Kızlarağası** (Head of Harem). There were different teams under the direction of one master. For each labour that had to be performed, their chambers were arranged in such a manner that a master or stewardess would sleep in the midst of a team of ten in order to prevent any discord. Now we will consider some examples to understand these teams and their duties.

Çaşnigir Usta (Master of Gastronomy): This team of stewardess and Cariyes would set the table and taste the food to prevent sultan and other members of the dynasty from being poisoned.

Kahveci Usta (Master of Coffee): This team would make coffee for the sultan, Sultan's mother and their guests and serve them. As you know, the tradition of serving Turkish coffee has also an important place in today's Turkey. The hosts serve Turkish coffee when an important and amiable guest comes.

İbriktar Usta (Master of Pitcher): As water had to be brought from outside, a small pitcher was used while washing the hands and feet by pouring water for them, especially as it was necessary for abdest (Islamic ritual for washing before praying) five times a day.

Kilerci Usta (Master of Stocks): This team was responsible from the drinks, fruit and whet in the stores. They would work with the team of Team of Gastronomy, which were serving the food.

Kutucu Usta (Master of Caretaking): They would help sultans, other members of the dynasty and favourites while they were having bath and preparing all the utensils necessary during the bath.

Külhancı Usta (Stoker Master): The stokers were responsible from the heating and cleaning of Turkish baths. Helping the favouites that would spend the night with Sultan to have bath was also their duty.

Hastalar Ustası (Master of Sick): This team was responsible from the health of all the people in harem. They would look after the sick, perform midwifery and make abortions. Wet nurses (Daye) and babysitters, that were taken into harem to suckle and take care of the babies, worked in this team. Abortions were especially important since the reign of Sultan Ahmet I (17th. century) until the reign of Sultan Abdülaziz (19th. century), because at that time princes were not allowed to have children. For that reason any pregnancy caused by them was immediatly prevented. Only the prince that managed to be sultan acquired this right. Princes were not sent to various regions of the empire as governors, as it used to be but were leading a confined kind of

Caring of an Harem Lady

Baby nursing Harem ladies

prisoner's life in the palace.

As in many other subjects, there were exceptions to this, too. For instance Abdülhamid I (1775-89) prevented one of his women to have abortion and let his daughter Sultana Dürrüsehvar to be born. Abdülhamid raised his daughter secretly outside the palace and could be able to bring her to palace only after becoming sultan. In the palace, Daye (wet nurses) of the sultans had a very special place. They were either from famous families or an appropriate woman who had recently given birth would be taken into service in harem. Except for the members of the dynasty, only the wet nurses and the babysitters could hold the children of the sultan in their arms, because they were seen as the people close to dynasty. Sultan Mehmed the Conqueror had given so much money and presents to his Wet Nurse Hundi Hatun that she could donate four prayer rooms, two of them in Istanbul and two of them in Edirne. Sultan Süleyman the Magnificent was so generous towards his Wet Nurse that she could have Daye Hatun Mosque built in Istanbul.

Hazinedar Master (Treasurer Master): All of the private servants of the sultan were called "hazinedar" (treasurers). A team consisting of about 15-20 stewardess and maids (cariyes) with the Treasurer Master as their head, would only perform the private service of sultan. The jobs of Treasurer Master and her four assistants were the most favourite in harem. This head of the team consisting of five people were at the same responsible from all of the treasure rooms of harem and treasurer master was the only person who possessed the keys of all treasures. The members of the team would be personally chosen among the maids (cariye) by the sultan. Treasurer master and her four assistants would wait in front of the door of the sultan's room when he was in. Only the one who was the master could go into the sultan's room without needing a permission. Because these masters were work-ing very close to sultan, they knew many private issues. When the sultan died or was dethroned, they were also dismissed from their jobs. Then they would usually live in the old palace with the former sultan's mother, wives, children and sisters. The new sultan would bring his mother, wives and other members of dynasty to harem, have them settled in and choose a new and reliable team of treasurers among the female personnel. Of course, he would take the recommendations of Kızlar Ağası and masters.

It happened that a sultan would like one of the girls in the treasurer team and make her one of his favourites, because only those who had managed to pass the cultural and physical election and who could be efficient, could work so close to the sultan.

Kethüda Kadın (Chief Housekeeper): Unfortunately there are not much information about Kethüda Kadın in the archives. As far as it is known the most cultured, most ex-perienced, the oldest servant who had done longer service would be appointed to this position. According to the observations that the daughters of latest sultans narrated, they were the most efficient servant of Sultan's mother and they would arrange all celebrations and activi-ties. During the celebrations of the Feast of Sacrifices or Feast of Rama-dan or during a ceremony, Kethüda Kadın would stand in front of the servants as the one who arranged it. For her to wear at official ceremonies and celebrations, a velvet or silk caf-tan would be given to her by the sul-tan. A silver scepter and a seal gi-ven to her would symbolize the privileged position of Kethüda Kadın among all masters.

Every night about 15 or 20 maids, under the supervision of two stewardess, would keep guard in harem. They would gather in the Saloon of the Sultan, walk along the courtyards and corridors in teams of two or three and provide the night to pass quiet and calm. Their duty would begin with the latest prayer of the day, and last until the morning call for prayer.

All of the servants would be committed to work in harem for nine years. With the end of this time, they were given an itik -or an azad-name- (a report of freedom). Most of them would return this report and say that they wanted to go on with their duty for some more time. Those who depart would keep the azadname until they died, and some were even buried with it hanging from their necks. According to the service they had done, they would be given a ring and an earring ornamented with gems, a golden watch, silver utensils and food in memory of palace.

Servants were not only educated about the works they would be doing but also about reading Koran and following the rules of Islam,

Harem Lady

Birth scene in Harem

A Prince and his mother

but we understand from the narration of an observation told from the period of Sultan Reşad (1909 - 18), that some exceptions were seen. One day the sultan called the teacher who had recently come to palace and warned him: "Whoever does not perform the divine prayers or fast, I will not give up freely the bread and salt that I give them." Upon this the teacher, Safiye Hanım, hanged a warning notice on the door of the class: "Those that do not perform the divine prayers or fast cannot attend the lesson." This event also shows us how important the education of personnel was. Except for Koran, they were educated in music, singing, knitting and embroidery to the degree of their willingness and ability.

The sultan would have no relation with most of the women that constituted the majority of harem's people. As they were considered to be the "ayak takımı" (low ranking members) of harem, they would almost never come across each other. When an encounter with the sultan was inevitable, it was almost impossible for their eyes to meet as they bowed down to their feet. Any way the intelligent and beautiful girls, appropriate for the sultan, would be chosen by a special team and appointed to his close service. For instance, Sultan Osman III (1754-57) preferred to keep away from music, fun and women to the degree of hatred. When he became sultan at the age of 55, he dismissed musicians, singers, and dancers from harem. He had pieces of iron nailed under his shoes to prevent coming across any maids while he was wandering around in harem and ordered anybody who heard his footsteps to disappear from his sight. This occasion has no generality, but it is illuminating concerning the views of the sultans about the maids. Because Sultan Osman III had spent 55 years of his life in dim and damp rooms under observance, by the time he ascended to throne he was to much wearied out both physically and psychologically.

Harem Ladies in turkish bath (Hamam)

THE ELECT WOMEN

As we mentioned earlier, a muslim man, who is in an available financial position could marry four women at most, but when we look at the archives in Topkapı Palace, we see that the sultans were being with more than four women. For that reason, we have to divide these women that we call elect into categories. Just as the maids in harem were arranged according to a hierarchical relationship, there was a definite classification among these elect women. The ones to come the first were the **four wives of the Sultan (Kadınefendi),** then came the **blissfuls (ikbal)** and finally the **favourites (gözde).** A Sultan could have a marital relationship only with the women in these three groups. We will deal with the three classification of women closely.

Gözde (The Favourites): They were the youngest among the elect women and their ages were between 17 and 23. The sultan himself would usually choose them, but they could also be given as a present or recommended by the Vizier, the Sultan's mother, his sisters and other high officers. It is not easy to determine their number but it changed with each sultan, but it is possible to say from the evidences we have got that they ranged from 4 to 10, because only when a favourite gave birth, was she taken into official records. A maid chosen to be a favourite would be first handed over to Hazinedar Usta (treasurer master). After she was given a room in the Gözdeler Odası (apartment of the favourites) and a few maids under her service, she would be taught how to behave the sultan and the servants that worked in his room, because being a Favourite meant rising to one of the important status in harem. With this promotion, a favourite achieved the chance

of becoming Sultan's mother, i.e. the most powerful woman of one of the greatest and most powerful empires in history.

When the sultan wants to spend the night with one of the favourites, he would tell his decision to Kızlar Ağası (The Head of Harem) and then the necessary procedures according to the traditions of palace would be carried out. The chosen favourite would be washed well in Hamam (Turkish bath) by **Külhancı Usta** (Stoker Master) and nice perfumes would be put onto her body. The sultan would send precious presents to the favourite and pay a brief visit to her.

One difference of the favourite, that separated her from other women was that, in case they would not give birth or were not liked by the sultan any longer, they could be made to marry the high officers of the state. This meant that the position of the favouites in relation to the dynasty was not yet strong, only when they gave birth could they be promoted and enter the class of İkbals (blissfuls).

A Favourite

İkbal (blissfuls): İkbals would be considered as the members of the dynasty as they have given birth to the child of the sultan. They would never be married to anybody else. In the records we see the first ikbal during the reign of Sultan Mustafa II (1695 - 1703), there is no information about their existence earlier. A sultan could have about 6 or 8 ikbals. The one with the highest rank was called **Baş İkbal** (the head of blissfuls) and the others would be numbered as the second, third, fourth, etc. İkbal. All of them were addressed as "Hanımefendi" (Madam), lived in rooms of their own and were given maids under their service.

The promotion in the ranks of İkbals was possible if they gave birth to a son, if an ikbal of higher rank died or the sultan divorced one of his wives. It was sometimes seen that a sultan could be fond of one of his favourites more than his wives. For instance Sultan Abdülmecid showed more affection to his second ikbal Serefaz Hanım than his sixth ikbal Naciye Hanım, who he also loved very much, but he caused jealousy among his other women. This jealousy that was sometimes secret, sometimes overt had occasionally caused fatal intrigues. However, ikbals could never manage to be as powerful and as respected as Kadınefendi (the wives of the sultan).

Kadınefendi (Wives of the sultan): The number of wives of the sultan ranged between 4 and 8. These were generally the women that the sultan married earliest. They had ranks like baş kadın efendi (senior wife of the sultan), the second, the third, etc. wife among themselves. As we mentioned earlier, they were once in the status of slaves and were made wife to the sultan without getting married. Although it is rare, it was observed that some sultans set the Kadınefendis they loved so much free to be able to marry and married them as free

Ladies of Harem at the banks of the Golden Horn

woman. Furthermore, especially during the Foundation and Development Eras, sultans got married without wedding ceremonies. Perhaps it was thought that preparing a wedding appropriate for a palace for each of the 4 or 8 women would be extravagence, they contented with a simple ceremony with family members. Some sultans were so loyal to their wives that they kept away from favourites or Happy Ones. Sultan Murad III (1574 - 95) and Sultan Ahmed III (1709 - 30) were among the ones who liked variety. Most of the privilege in harem was of course given to the wives of the sultans. They could go out of harem more often and more freely and could get more wage from the treasury. As well as the number of maids, the amount of annual food and precious clothes given to them were more than the others. In the earlier periods of the empire, they could live in the states with their sons.

The fact that sultans could not behave as arbitrary as they are thought to do, but had to stick to traditions and customs, is quite explicitly reflected in an event that happened to Sultan Mustafa III (1557 - 74): "Sultan Mustafa had a secret love affair with a slave named "Rifat Kadın" outside harem, living most probably with a family close to the palace. When one day he wanted to have her in his harem, he told his written order to his Vizier with these words: "My Vizier, let nobody ask any questions as to where this cariye (Rifat Kadın) came from. As you know we kept it as a secret to this day. Arrange it so that those who accompany her should not say anything. They should not enter through the main entrance, it is crowded and there are too many eunuch guards, it is better if they entered through the more calm Simsirlik Gate." Upon this, sadrazam sent this answer: "I think those who accompany the cariye

The rooms of favourites and Courtyard

cannot hold their tongues, but will tell where she comes from. I believe this will be a great risk. "But the Sultan wrote this note beneath the Vizier's and sent it back: "In that case, order them to swear and say, when they are asked, that they do not know anything but only the Vizier does." It is clear that even a sultan suffers great difficulties when he wants to act contrary to traditions.

There was always a rivalry due to sovereignty struggle among wives. Especially if more than one women had sons, each of them wanted to make her son sultan and her self to be the most powerful woman of the empire, Sultan's mother. Uniting with the political struggles of its day, this motive to be the sovereign generally became the source of fatal intrigues of the palace.

Jealousy was most frequently

observed among the wives of the sultan. The Senior wife of Sultan Mehmed IV (1648 - 86) Gülnuş Kadın was a slave from Crete and she had managed to attract the attention of the sovereign in a short period of time and gave two sons to him. The sultan was generally very loyal to Gülnuş Kadın and would rarely be with other women, but when Gülnuş Kadın understood tha a favourite named Gülbeyaz was about to steal his heart, she had a picnic organized as soon as possible and pushed Gülbeyaz secretly down the rocks. Gülnus Kadın used to get on well with her mother-in-law, Turhan Sultan. When Turhan Sultan died in 1684, Gülnuş Kadın became the absolute woman dominant both in harem and in the empire, but she never intervened in politics.

Entrance to the rooms of the Sultans mother

SULTAN'S MOTHER

Validesultan (Sultan's mother): She was the absolute woman sovereign of both harem and the empire. With one or two exceptions, all of the sultans were very dependent on their mothers, and treasured them more than anything else. The requests and opinions of the mother were always taken into consideration. In fact she would determine and direct everything that happened in harem. Even the journeys arranged for fun would be organized according to her wishes. The biggest rooms, after those of the sultans, were spared for them. Of course, the largest number of maids were at her service. Her sons would give their mothers a lot of money and farms that brought too much income, and these were run by the mediation of "Valide Kethüda"s (helpers of of the Mother).

Sultan's mothers were more experienced in political and palace life than their sons, because they would come to the palace at the ages between 8 and 14, and after being educated here, despite the many difficulties and intrigues, they would climb up the degrees of harem step by step until they became the wife of the sultan. They would gain their first experience of active political life at the side of the sultans. When one of their sons became the sultan - mothers would any way have a great part in this -, they would take on an active role in politics with their sons. Only a few of the Sultan's mothers stayed away from politics.

One of the most splendid celebrations of the empire was the Valide alayı (parade for Sultan's mother). This parade would be held 2 or 3 days earlier than the enthronement of the sultan (cülus). The new sultan would order his mother to be brought from the old palace to the harem of Topkapı Palace. A crowded group of states-

Detail of a wall painting in the saloon of Sultan's mother

Entrance to the rooms of Sultan's mother

Dome of the reception hall

men, masters, servents and army officers would accompany the parade from Beyazıt to **Bab-ı Hümayun** (Imperial Gate), the first gate of Topkapı Palace. Sultan Selim III (1789 - 1807) met his mother at the first garden of Topkapı Place, opened the door of pheaton, and after kissing her hand, accompanied her to harem and ended the parade.

Courtyard of the Sultans mother

27

BUYING SLAVES

There were definitely various ways of providing enough healthy, beautiful and young girls to do the labours of harem. During the Expansion Era, these were chosen among the slaves captured on the lands invaded, however when the development was completed and no new lands were any longer acquired, usually the governors of various regions gave girls that they bought from their estates as present to sultan. The sisters of sultan who started to live outside harem after they got married would give appropriate cariye's under their service to him as present.

The largest slave market of Middle East was Bagdat, next came most probably, the one in Istanbul.

Preeminently Circassian, Georgian and Abkhasian girls were bought for harem. Except for those that were given as presents, there were others that an officer who was in charge of buying slaves bought directly from the market.

The use of slaves within the empire was in the following manner: Slaves older than 20 would directly be servants.

Those between the ages of 5 and 7 would be brought up by their owners, educated according to their abilities, taught the traditions and customs, and prepared as a servant. If desired, they could be sold or given as present.

The most expensive slaves were the ones between 15 and 20 years of age and they would usually be brought up by the families close to the palace; Since the daughters of these families did not have the chance of becoming the wife of the sultan, at least the cariye's that they brought up themselves could be able to reach this honour. The best example to of this situation is the Senior Wife of Sultan Abdülhamid II (1876 - 1909), Nazikeda Hanım. This girl was from a noble Circassian family, and she was bought from a slave market and brought up by Ali Pasha. As soon as the sultan saw Nazikeda, a beautiful and welleducated girl, he solicited and took her into his harem.

When Ali Pasha and his wife, who were extremely proud that the slaves they brought up became the senior wife of the sultan, often went to visit her and wanted to greet her by bowing down to their feet, but Nazikeda would say: "I beg you!... You are the people who raised me up to this status, our mighty master permits us to kiss your hands, I'd like to have that honour." But neither Ali Pasha nor his wife would let her kiss their hands but contented with em-

Slave market in Istanbul

List of Servants

bracing her.

A great attention was paid to the health and physical appearances of the slaves. The unhealthy ones would be returned. If a slave had a family, an official writing, saying that they would not want anything more in return for their children and claim no rights on them, would be taken from them. The slaves would be given a new name as soon as they arrived harem. Usually the names of flowers would be preferred and until the names were memorized by everybody, they would carry them attached to their collars. After they were through with their jobs in harem and started to live outside it, it was not infrequent that they used their earlier names.

Today's people may not naturally be accustomed the notion of having slaves, however it will not be at all untrue to say that the notion of slavery in Ottomans showed characteristics close to the notion of adoption today. As there were annihilating wars more often and no institutions to heal the social ills these cause, many orphan children were sold at the slave markets. Some were even sold by their families due to poverty, because in this way they could make it possible for their children to be brought up by a rich family, or to have a career by being accepted to harem. We should not forget that all of the wives of the sultan and later Sultana's mother began their careers as slaves and rose to the most important status of the empire. With this narration, we do not aim at rejecting the existing tragic events among slaves, but our intention is to give a general information of within the framework of our subject. The biography of İbrahim Edhem Bey is typical one: In 1825, Hüsrev Pasha, a naval officer, bought four boys who were brought to Istanbul after the suppression of a insurrection in Kiosk Island. One of the was Edhem

Bey. Hüsrev Bey brought up the four boys and in 1829 he came to the presence of sultan and said that he wanted to have these children educated in France. With the approval of the sultan, the pioneer students were sent to France and were educated there. Returning from France, İbrahim Bey joined the army, then he became a minister and on the 5th. of February in 1877 he was promoted to be the Vizier. Then he worked as an ambassador and minister of Internal Affairs. He dien in 1885.

Festivities at the Golden Horn

Ladies of Harem outside Harem

FESTIVITIES IN HAREM

We have dealt with the people who constitute the essence of harem and their duties until this point. The people of harem were not only working and doing their duties, but their need to enjoy themselves was satisfied by the arrangement of various festivities without transcending the limits of ethic and tradition. As in other aspects of harem life, a special attention was paid to keep these entertainment within the limits of the prohibitions and allowances in Islam. The celebrations in harem must naturally be considered in two groups; religious ones and the ones made for the sake of enjoyment. Religious celebrations were, of course, of more importance, and other festivities were of various characteristics and frequency depending on the attitude of the sultan and the economical conditions of the country. Since the Foundation Era until the end of 17th. century, not much place and time was devoted to entertainment, but this was not the case during the Retension and Demolition Eras that lasted until 1922.

When the most important religious feast days of Islam, the Bairam of Sacrifices and Bairam of Ramadan came, harem would be wrapped with a divine atmosphere. Everyone was obliged either to fast or at least not to make it known that she was not fasting. This religious duty was not obligatory for the sick, for the pregnant women and the children. Various kinds of food would be distributed and sherbet would be offered to the people of harem. After iftar (dinner at Ramadan when Muslims broke their fasting), they would sit until sahur (meal at dawn in Ramadan) singing hymns and chatting. During the month of Ramadan clericgy man would come to direct the people in performing divine prayers and to preach them.

A woman dancer

Harem would look like a huge mosque with many rooms. Other religious Bairams would be celebrated with the same deep faith. Musical nights would always be organized in harem. "Sazende" (an orchestra) of maids would play Turkish Classical Music and the listeners would accompany them. Such kind of nights were organized a few times in a month and only the sultan, his mother, his wives, ikbals, his children and his sisters attended. The largest saloon of harem "Hünkar Salonu" (Saloon of the Sultan) was designed with this intention. If the sultan himself was a musician, a composer or a poet, these nights would be more meaningful. Playing and singing Turkish Classical Music with the members of family or group of friends is a tradition that still survives. More difficult and extensive arrangements were organized in accordance with the mentality of seclusion in harem. The best loved entertainment were the long trips into nature and shores of Golden Horn This name was, any way, given to this bay as the symbol of the golden times,. when a colourful and enjoyable life was led here by the Ottomans.

Many days earlier, tents were put up in the midst of nature and they were linked to each other with roads that were covered with clothes on each side. Every precaution was taken in order to prevent the women of harem from being seen by any stranger man. In the covered roads, which had a number reaching up to 50, they could enjoy themselves as they wished and watch the festivities, distant from the foreign eyes without being distrubed. Because the number of the people of harem was quite high, they would be brought to the entertainment area in groups. Those who found their names on the lists that were hanged on the wall in harem, would immediately wear their best dresses, get on to phaetons and set off in a hierarchical order under the supervision of chief eunuchs. The

entertainment area was a kind of fair place. They would spend days full of fun, playing music, singing, organizing sportive competitions and eating the best kind of sweets. This was a very enjoyable change for the women who spent most of their time confined in rooms and courtyards of harem. Except for these, festivities of high cost would be organized to celebrate births, marriages of the daughters of the sultans or circumcisions of the sons of the sultans. Oriental dances, acrobatic shows, shows of the dwarfs and puppet shows were the crucial parts of these ostentatious celebrations.

Various dance shows would be held, too, but these were not performed in the saloons of harem, each of which were ornamented with many verses from Koran, but were instead performed in other palaces, mansions or at the resting and entertainment areas called "Hasbahçe." During the Tulip Period (1718-30), these entertainment, which reached extreme limits, were arranged primarily at such places appropriate for entertainment like Sadabat, Şerefabat, Hüsrevabat and

Acrobats

Neşetabat. One of these dances which is still known at our day is **"Köçekçe,"** that is performed either by homosexuals or men in woman's clothes. Boys, at the ages of 7 and 8, would learn this dance and perform their abilities in groups unti they were 13 or 14. They had lon hair that reached their shoulders and wore vests of embroidered silk. Especially the gypsy dancers and dancers from Kiosk Island were very famous and desired. They usually used pseudo names like **"Taze Fidan"** (Fresh Nursling), **"Altın Top"** (Golden Ball) or **"Büyük Afet"** (Great Beauty). They danced at weddings, celebrations of circumcision and other feasts in all regions of the empire in return for money. Today, it is still possible to watch "Köçek" in Turkey.

Some of the sultans would also allow for dances that can be considered to be erotic according to the conditions of its day. A group of 12 women, whose dresses partially chiffon, would try to impress the audience with their agile dances. They would accompany their dances with the cymbals on their fingers. This kind of dances were seen within the last 100 or 150 years of the Ottomans.

In the 19th. century, with the changes in the cultural life that occurred under western influence, theater plays and operas began to be performed. During the reign of Sultan Abdülhamid II (1876 - 1909) theater plays were the most important artistic activity of the people of palace. Western composers and artists like Ayvazofsky had the opportunity to perform their art in the Ottoman Palace and created works, each one more beautiful than the other. The inclination towards the western culture in 19th. century found its place in the application of official architecture, and palaces and mosques started to be adorned with Baroque and Gothic Styles. Atatürk, on the other hand, with the changes he made, provided the society to join in this process of modernization that Ottomans began.

OUTSTANDING PERSONALITIES ROXELANE (HÜRREM SULTAN)

Roxelane was the first of the wives of the Sultans to make politics actively in the Ottoman history. Roxelane was brought to Istanbul at the age of approximately 14 or 17 after an expenditure made to Balkan Peninsula and she attracted attention with her intelligence and vigilant appearance, and was given to Sultan Süleyman the Magnificent (1520-66) as a present. Some sources assert that she was the daughter of a Russian priest, and some others assert her to be Italian or French in origin. Wherever she was from, she gained the appreciation of the Sultan with her pure white skin and meaningful looks, and was taken into his harem. When Roxelane, after becoming pregnant, wanted to leave harem, although it was against the traditions, Sultan Süleyman the Magnificent made her stay by marrying her. This behaviour showed her how much sultan valued her, and encouraged her. Sultan Süleyman had five wives until that day, and especially the mother of Şehzade Mustafa, Mahidevran Hanım, did not like this situation at all. A rivalry that was difficult to avert began among Mahidevran Hanım and Roxelane. With the help of continuous interventions of Hafsa Sultan, mother of the Sultan, an overt struggle was prevented. After the death of Hafsa Sultan, Roxelane attained the absolute hegemony of harem; because meanwhile she gave birth to two more sons and a daughter, and became the Senior wife that Sultan could not give up. Roxelane behaved faster and made her rival, Mahidevran Hanım, sent to Manisa where her son was the governor, at once. İbrahim Pasha, the most powerful Grandvizier of Ottoman history, was on duty then. İbrahim Pasha had gained so much power that he was acting as a second Sultan. When this Grandvizier, who was of Greek origin, had the splendid İbrahim Pasha Palace built at today's Sultanahmet Square, all the people of Palace began to say that this was much bigger and more glamorous than harem, where Sultan lived. Roxelane knew that İbrahim Pasha was on the side of the son of her rival Mahidevran Hanım, Şehzade Mustafa, therefore influencing the sultan, she had İbrahim Pasha murdered. Instead of him, she made her son-in-law Rüstem Pasha, who would remain loyal to her until his death, Grandvizier.

By that time Sultan Süleyman was 60 years old and under the total influence of his beloved wife Roxelane. It would not be too difficult for her to eliminate the greatest rival of her sons. She wrote a letter to Shah of Persia, Tahmasp from Şehzade Mustafa's mouth, as if he wanted help from the Persian Shah to dethrone his father and promised for some land in return. The answer came soon, and Persian Shah as well as accepting the offer, wanted more land. When the letter was given to the elderly Sultan, he could not believe his eyes, because as his son would naturally come to throne after his death, he did not understand why he betrayed him especially with their eternal enemy, Persia, and felt very miserable.

Sultan thought of punishing his son, but Şehzade Mustafa was hastily strangled near Konya in 1553. Upon this event sultan sensed that something was being imposed upon him, but it was impossible for him to solve the intrigue

Roxelane, daughter of a russian (?) priest

any longer. However, meanwhile Janissaries rebelled because they thought Rüstem Pasha to be responsible for the death of Şehzade Mustafa. Upon this incident, Sultan dismissed Rüstem Pasha from his post, but by the help of excessive requests of Roxelane, Rüstem Pasha restored to his position. Meanwhile Roxelane's youngest son, Şehzade Cihangir, fell ill and died, because of the sorrow he felt for the death of his beloved step-brother Mustafa. The way to the throne was opened to Roxelane's two sons: Şehzade Bayezit and Şehzade Selim II were left against each other.

When Roxelane died unexpectedly at the age of 54 in 1558, Süleyman the Magnificent had a mausoleum built for her in the garden of Süleymaniye Mosque. Her life could not be long enough for her to be the Sultan's mother, who she wished to be perhaps all through her life, but she found the chance of determining the political life more than she ought to at the side of her elderly husband who was so much devoted to her and used it as much as she could. Both of them had poetic inspirations and wrote poems for each other. In a line, Sultan Süleyman expressed his passion for Roxelane as if he was confessing: "Even when I am perform the divine prayers, I cannot think of anything but my Hürrem." When we consider the fact that a muslim should not think of anything other than God while praying, we can say that Roxelane was deified as a goddess in the eyes of Süleyman the Magnificent and this goddess found freedom that no other wife of the sultans could dream of, and determined the fate of one of the greatest empires of history. No other slave could influence a sultan that much and manage to make him marry her. Still all of these could not succeed in preventing her sons from having to reap the bitter fruits that Roxelane sow with her ambition for sovereignty.

Şehzade Selim II and his brother Bayezit were the two heirs of the empire. With the death of their mother, a deep distrust occurred between them. Şehzade Selim II, towards whom Roxelane felt more sympathetic, was supported by Rüstem Pasha and janisaries. Bayezit, on the other hand, had the weak support of the villager and spahees. In order to bring an ultimate solution to the struggle for the throne, the two brothers faced each other near Konya in 1559. Şehzade Bayezit was defated and ran away with his four sons to Persia and asked for refuge from Tahmasb. In 1561, Beyazit and his sons were given back in return for 300.000 gold and killed. When his father Süleyman the Magnificent died in 1566, Şehzade Selim II, having emerged with victory from the chain of intrigues that his mother started, became the sultan of the greatest empire of the world; greatest because during the reign of Süleyman the Magnificent, the treasury was filled, the land of the empire spread over three continents and reached an area of 24 billion m^2 that it would never ever reach again.

Harem ladies in the living-room

KÖSEM SULTAN

During the Ottoman history, which lasted 600 years, many events worthy of being mentioned took place, but among these we chose only those events and people that reflect the characteristics of both harem and the empire. One of the most well-known people of the empire was "Mahpeyker Sultan." This woman, whose better known name was "Kösem Sultan," was one of the wives of Sultan Ahmed (1603 - 17), who had the Blue Mosque built. Although it was not decided upon whether she was Greek or Bosnian, it was known that she was the daughter of a Christian priest. She had all the prerequisites to be dominant in harem; beauty, kindness, attraction and intelligence. She attracted the attention of Ahmed I as soon as she arrived harem. Moreover, when she gave birth to Şehzade Murad IV, İbrahim, Süleyman and Kasım, she became the most respected woman of the sultan that he could not give up. When Ahmed I died unexpectedly at a young age, and when first his brother Mustafa I, then Osman II ascended to throne, Kösem Sultan was sent to the old palace with her children due to the traditions. After six years passed, when her son Murad IV (1623 - 39) became sultan, she returned to harem as the Sultan's mother with the accompaniment of a parade. She managed to be on the agenda of the political life and harem as an intrigant and powerful Sultan's mother until the end of her life.

Because her son became sultan at the age of 12, she took the administration into her hands and used it as she wished. She secured her position by establishing good relationships with janisaries. When Murad IV died, her other son İbrahim (1639 - 47) became sultan. Sultan (Insane) İbrahim had, most probably, a psychological illness,

psycho neurosis - according to the scientists of our day -, therefore again Kösem Sultan took the administration in her hands. By giving him slaves, each more beautiful than the other, as present, she made him spend his time with enjoyment, and behaved as she wished in administration. However, the wives of Sultan İbrahim were reacting against her arbitrary administration and consequently, having the sultan on their side, they had her exiled from harem. Even though her son wanted to sent her to exile, as Kösem Sultan had gained important supporters with bribe and promises, her supporters dethroned the sultan by rebelling against him. Instead of him, they made İbrahim's 7 years old son, Mehmed IV (1647-86) sultan. Finding this opportunity, Kösem Sultan returned to harem at once. There was only one obstacle before her regaining the administration: the mother of Mehmed IV and her daughter-in-law Turhan Sultan. Kösem Sultan planned to dethrone her 7 years old grandson and bring Süleyman II, whose mother was

more silent and preferred to remain at the background, to the throme, but before she could actualize her plan, Turhan Sultan learned about the plan and had Kösem Sultan, who held the politics of the empire in her hands for 28 years, strangled? In her room (1651). The most striking and rarest ambition of sovereignty of the Ottoman Era that could not be controlled came to an end.

Kösem Sultan was an intelligent and ambitious slave, who played the leading role in many bloody intrigues, but she could not save herself from being the victim of an intrigue she started. Despite everything, it is necessary to mention that if sovereignty was not in question, she had a humane side. Every year she would visit prisons and set those who were there due to their debts free by paying their debts. She would also make their daughters and girls marry and provide for their needs. Except these, it is known that she had many madrasahs, fountains and mosques built.

Detail of the Sultan's mother room

MARA (DESPINA)

As we mentioned earlier, marrying noble women was a part of Ottoman policy before Sultan Mehmed the Conqueror (1451 - 81). It is possible to see how tolerant Ottomans were about religions other than Islam, compared to the struggles between sects today.

The most interesting example of this is the biography of the lives of Serbian king Georg Braskovich and the daughter of his wife Irene Komnenos, Mara (Despina). Mara, who was born in 1419, was made to marry Murad II to provide peace between Ottomans and Serbs. Usually the non-muslim foreign brides changed their religion to Islam, but Mara was one of the brides who did not change their religions. For instance the second wife of Sultan Murad II decided to become muslim after she was impregnated and she gave birth to Sultan Mehmed the Conqueror from this pregnancy.

When Sultan Murad II died in 1451, his son Mehmed II, who came to throne, offered his step mother Mara to get married with a high officer, because Mara had gained the confidence of the Ottomans and was working as a missionary between East and West. The Emperor of Bizans also wanted to marry her but Mara refused his proposal and told Sultan that she wanted to go back to Serbia. Upon this, Sultan Mehmed II gave her a high amount of money and sent her to Serbia accompanied by soldiers. Mara, who had an ambitious personality, went into a sovereignty struggle for the Serbian throne with her brother. When she fell into difficulty, in 1457 she took refuge in Istanbul, that was conquered by her step son Sultan Mehmed the Conqueror by that time. From that time on, Mara, the widowed Christian wife of a muslim sultan, worked as the most authorized political representative of the Orthodox Church for years. During this period she helped Orthodox-Christian societies and her decision had been influential in the election of Patriarch. When Sultan Mehmed the Conqu-eror invaded Serbia, he gave her profitable farms and a lot of money. When she died in 1487 at 68 years of age, she was buried into the garden of Komca Monastery in Strunica.

Ladies with long full coat (Ferace)

Sultans wife and servant

HATİCE SULTAN

Hatice Sultan was one of the daughters of sultans with the most colourful personalities. She was the daughter of Sultan Murad V (1876) who could reign only for 93 days due to his psychological illness. After him his brother Abdülhamid II (1876 - 1909) came to throne and establishe a dictatorial regime, and Murad V was doomed to live an isolated life with his wives and children at Çırağan Palace. After the colourful palace life which lasted 93 days, a life full of disappointments and contempt began for his most lively and intelligent daughter, Hatice Sultan, too.

Hatice Sultan was so beautiful as to attract all the attentions to herself. She was receiving a very good education despite the prisoner life she and her sisters and brothers were forced to live. In the following years, although she came to the age of 31, neither she nor her other sisters were made to marry by their uncle, Abdülhamid II. She had sent messages to her uncle many times and told him her desire to get rid off this imprisonment whatever it might worth, even if it meant marrying a castrated man.

Upon this, the sultan had all the sisters and brothers brought to Yıldız Palace on the condition that they would never return to Çırağan Palace, but although many months passed by, no improvement concerning their marriages could be seen. Meanwhile the daughters of the sultan were getting married with high officers one after the other. When Hatice Sultan informed the sultan about her desire to get married again, he got her dowry prepared at once and chose a sordu, a middle rank officer, as suitable to be her husband. In order to make him appropriate to be the husband of a sultana, he was given the title Pasha and was promoted as a for-

mality, but the fact that Vasıf Bey was not noble, had a huge body and full and long moustache seemed so irritating to Hatice Sultan that, she did not want to share the same bed with her husband since the very first night of their marriage. The house they lived in was in Ortaköy, next to the house of Naile Sultan, the most beloved daughter of the sultan. Although she was not as beautiful and attractive as Hatice Sultan, the sultan had his own daughter marry the handsome son of a famous Pasha, Kemaleddin Pasha. Hatice Sultan was feeling a great hatred towards her uncle, Sultan Abdülhamid II, because of the slave life he forced her, her father and her family to live, and the marriage that dishonoured her.

Hatice Sultan took the revenge of the sufferings she and her family were made to endure by writing letters to and tempting the husband of Naime Sultan, the best loved daughter of Sultan Abdülhamid II. When this affair was found out in 1904, it created a shock in the palace. Kemaleddin Pasha, who dishonoured the favourite daughter of the sultan by betraying her, was exiled to Bursa after all of his title were taken from him. Meanwhile,

Murad V, who felt very miserable for the sensational revenge of his daughter, became more ill and died within a few months. When the Second Constitution was declared in 1908, Kemaleddin Bey returned to his earlier position. Although he proposed Hatice Sultan by official means, he was continuously refused. Hatice Sultan married Rauf Bey who was working at External Affairs in 1909. Two children were the offspring of this marriage, a son and a daughter.

When the Republic of Turkey was founded in 1923, all of the members of the dynasty were sent out of the country (1924).

Hatice Sultan went to Beirut with her children and lived there suffering many problems until she died, because the husbands of sultans could stay in the country if they wished. They were given this right to choose, because they became the member of the dynasty through marriage, and Rauf Bey was one of the son-in-laws who chose to stay. In fact he was sending alimony enough to live on to Hatice Sultan and his children, but when he was dismissed from his job, Hatice Sultan had to spend her last years in bitter poverty.

Woman resting after bath

PLAN OF HAREM

1. Vehicle Gate
2. Gate with lockers
3. Tower Gate
4. Tower of Justice
5. Sultan's horse slope
6. Entrance of Harem
7. The personnel room of the male slave gate keepers
8. Turkish bath of eunuchs
9. Courtyard of eunuchs
10. Prayer room for eunuchs
11. Dormitory of eunuchs
11.a. Lavatory of eunuchs
12. The room of the male slave gate keepers
13. Rooms of the heads of harem
14. Room of jesters
15. Room of dwarfs
16. Room of Treasurer Master
17. Gate of Harem
18. The sentry place of eunuchs
19. The door of Goldenroad
20. The gate of the couryard of Sultan's mother
21. The entrance for slaves
22. The room of masters
23. Pharmacy
24. Courtyard of slaves
25. The rooms of wives of the sultan
26. Staircase of the hospital
27. Courtyard of slaves
28. Gate of the laundry
29. Laundry
30. The kitchen and the rooms of the hospital
31. The rooms of slaves
32. The rooms of sick-attendants
33. The rooms of slaves
33.a. Lavatory of slaves
34. Laundry
35. Kitchen
36. Food store
37. Turkish bath for slaves
38. Entrance of the pavilion of Sultan's mother
39. The room of Lady Housekeeper
40. Saloon of Sultan's mother
41. Chamber of Sultan's mother
42. Room of Sultan's mother where she performed divine service
43. Entrance
44. Kitchen of Sultan's mother
45. The waiting room of Sultan's mother
46. Sentry place
47. Turkish bath of Sultan's mother
48. Turkish bath of the sultan
49. The room of the stoker
50. The chamber of Abdülhamid I
51. The room of Selim III

52. Courtyard with pool
53. The villa of Osman III
54. Saloon of the Sultan
55. Saloon with a fountain
56. Saloon with a fireplace
57. The waiting room of Murad III
58. The room of Murad III
59. The reading room of Ahmed I
60. The fruit room of Ahmed III
61. Classrooms
62. Pool

63. The courtyard of favourites
64. Goldenroad
64.a. The rooms of favourites
65. Kitchen
66. The rooms of "blissfuls"
67. The treasury room
68. The prayer room of Harem
69. Passage
70. Room with mirrors

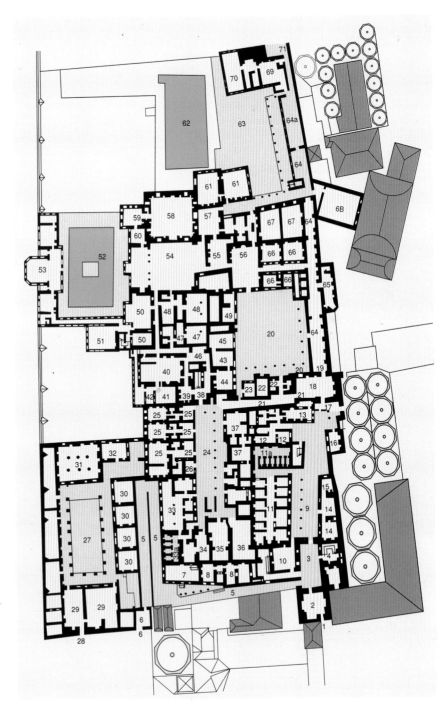

Bab-u Selam, 2. gate of Topkapı Palace

HAREM GUIDE

The main entrance of harem is the gate from which visitors are taken in today. It is called **"Araba Kapısı"** (l) (= Vehicle Gate), because people used to enter by pheatons through it in the past. On this entrance gate, there is a inscription written during the reign of Sultan Murad III which says that an extensive restoration was made here in 1587. Harem, that was destroyed many times by earthquakes and fires, was repaired for a few times. Moreover, each sovereign had some new sections added according to need, and consequently the complicated and incongruent architectural structure that has no definite style occurred. Just after the entrance, the second gate **"Dolap Kapı"** (2) (= Locker Gate) comes. The section between the two gates is called **"Dolaplı Kubbe"**

(= Dome with Lockers), because in the past there were lockers into which documents about eunuchs were hidden on each side of the place. The following verse from Koran is written on this gate: "Our supreme God, who opens all the doors to us! We wish you to

open the most blessed of doors, too."

The third gate is **"Kule Kapısı"** (3) (= Tower Gate), because there is the entrance of the Tower of Justice just on the right side of it. On the

ground floor of the Tower of Justice just on the right side of it. On the ground floor of the tower, courts and meetings of divan (council) were held. Above the entrance the following verse from Koran that praises justice can be read: "Distributing justice for an hour in life is more important than worshipping for nothing."

On the same gate it is inscribed: "Only God is worthy of worshipping and Muhammed is his emissary." (In Arabic: La İlahe illallah, Muhammedin Resulallah)

Exactly across this gate, there is the prayer room where eunuchs performed their divine service. Above it were the rooms of the

personnel of **"Baş Kapı Gulamı"** (= The Male Slaves at the Main Entrance) who came right after "Kızlar Ağası" (Agha of Girls) in the hierarchy. When we pass through the third gate, we come to a large courtyard, 60m. long. On the left there is the two storied dormitory of eunuchs and across it there are the rooms of dwarfs and jesters whose duties were to entertain the sultan.

A little farther on the left there is another gate that opens to the rooms of "Baş Kapı Gulamı". On this gate there is a verse again taken from Koran, and obviously written there with the intention of making

eunuchs get on well with each other: "Undoubtedly all believers are brothers. When they fall into discord, make peace among them and make them get on well with each other."

In this courtyard, we can see the best examples of 17th. century ceramics art. The last gate on the left opens to the rooms of "Kızlar Ağası" (19) and the following inscription is written on it:

"We greet you all, you are welcome, and stay there forever." The fourth gate at the end of the courtyard is the main gate of harem (17). Even the eunuchs could not pass through this door without permission. From that point on the private life of sultan and his family had begun. The verse of the Koran on this door reminds the rules to be

obeyed when one is entering a foreign house. "You believers! Ask for permission when you enter the houses that do not belong to you and greet the household as you enter. This behaviour will be better for you."

Through the main gate of harem, you enter a little section which has three doors (19, 20, 21) opening to it and where there are two

Venetian mirrors. This the ultimate point where eunuchs mount guard. Next to the mirror on the left there is **"Cümle Kapısı"** (21) (= People's Gate) and the inscription on it is the same as the one on Dolap Kapı.

Through the door in the middle (20) you enter "Valide Sultan Taşlığı" (Courtyard of Sultan's mother) and through the one on the right you come to **"Altın Yol"** (Golden Road) and go on to the pavilion of the sultan.

Through the door on the left you enter **"Cariye Koridoru"** (21) (Corridor of Female Slaves). The long marble bank that attracts the attention here is for the meal brought from

the kitchen to be put here. Eunuchs would bring the meal so far and after they left it here and withdrew, the personnel of "Çaşnigir" (= gastronomy) team would serve it to harem.

At the end of the corridor, just before turning right, on the right there are rooms of masters (22) and pharmacy (20) that have doors opening to courtyard. When you turned right and entered through the door (38) you come to "Valide Sultan Salonu" (40) (Saloon of Sultan's mother). One of the two rooms that can be seen on the left is the chamber of Sultan's mother (41) and the other is her

praying room (42). Right next to these rooms were the rooms of "Kadınefendis" (25) (= The wives of sultan), quite close to their mother-in-law's.

As soon as you entered the saloon of Sultan's mother, the wall paintings which are of Western origin on the dome attract the attention. These were painted in the 19th. century on the paintings of earlier times that faded out. In the apartment of Sultan's mother, there is a guest room, a dining room, a chamber, a hamam (Turkish bath), a toilet, a reading room and a praying room. These are both at the center of harem and had views

opening to Haliç.

Through the door next to the china vase on the left you can go into "Hünkar Hamamı" (48) (Turkish bath of the sultan) that has three parts: Dressing room, massage room and bathroom. A caged corner attracts the attention in the last room. The sultan used to lock himself behind this cage while he was having a bath and thus had his bath in safety against any attempt of assassination, because he could be defenseless during his bath. On the way to "Hünkar Salonu" (54) (Saloon of the Sultan) an old Ottoman toilet can be seen on the left. As well as coffee, this kind of toilet was also seen and adopted by the Europeans during the Siege of Vienna in the 16th. century. Right after here the biggest saloon of harem, "Hünkar Salonu" (54)

comes. Here the apartment of Sultan's mother ends and that of the sultan begins. As well as dances, music and shows of the jesters were performed here, official congratulations and religious activities are thought to be held here. Just across the entrance there is a splendid box especially made of baldahin, a special kind of wood, for sultan to sit. The places reserved for Sultan's mother, his wives and the "happy ones" are seen on its right. The balcony on the right side of the sultan was spared for the sazendes (musicians) of harem and the ways up to it are on the back of the mirrors on the right and left. Its wooden carvings are in Rococo-Baroque style and were made in the 18th. century during the reign of Osman III. The Delft Chinas, with blue patterns on white, were brought specially from Europe. This saloon is ornamented with verses from Koran written on Delft Chinas. One of the verses from Koran reads:

"God is undoubtedly the creator and friend of human beings. God protects them from ills and does them favour. But those without faith, whose friend is Satan, are absolutely diverted from favours and led towards ills."

Although they do not have definite documents in their hands, many native and foreign writers claim that Ottomans used to arrange entertainment contrary to traditions and customs in this saloon, however,

its closeness to the apartment of Sultan's mother and many verses from Koran in the saloon refute such kind of baseless claims.

As we mentioned earlier many sultans had many rooms added or pulled down. In the next room (57), it is possible to observe this incongruent architecture on the curvature of the walls. We can also see two cylinders, that can revolve around its small axis, installed on the two corners of the walls at this place and other rooms, as well as

special holes made for lamps. These were put by unequaled Mimar Sinan in order to be able to observe the possible curvatures on the walls that might be caused by earthquakes. When there was a movement on the walls, cylinders would get stuck and not revolve any longer. In such cases the architects would take the necessary precautions and prevent a probable collapse.

When you go left from this room, you enter the room of Murad III, which was repaired in the fifties and where there is one of the most beautiful domes of harem. In this room there is a fountain on the left wall, which was made not only to make the room cool, but also to be

pictures of various flowers and fruits under the influence of Tulip Period. Going back the same way, you come to a place (57) where there are the marble cylinders. On the left at the exit there are the two classrooms for sons of the sultans (61). The sons of the sultans were being educated here until the age of 16. Primarily Islamic theology, philosophy, mathematics, foreign languages and geography were taught. These classrooms are quite beautiful and attractive with their ceiling paintings, colourful glasses of the windows and Chinas. The ornamentation of the dome in the first room is a rare art of work made by embroidery on linen. The flower patterns on the Chinas of the second room are duplicated on the coloured glasses of the room. The fountains on the sides of the windows are installed both to make the room cool and prevent the echoing of the voices.

When you come out of the classrooms, you come to an open area where there is **"Gözdeler Taşlığı"** (63) (The courtyard of the

used during secret talks to prevent the echoing of the voices. On the right of the entrance, a corner designed for talking under a baldahin - a special kind of wood - box and in the middle of it a brazier attracts the attentions. The team of Strokers would put the charcoals they provided into it and make the rooms warm.

When you go farther from this room you come to the reading room of Ahmed I (59). In this room, there are more verses from Koran written on china than there are in other rooms. You can go to the dining and fruit room of Ahmed III (60) from the left of this room. All of the walls of the room are ornamented with

45

Favourites). There is **"Gözdeler Dairesi"** (64, 64a) (The apartment of Favourites), two storied and wooden building, on the southern end of the courtyard. At the furthest end of the building, just across it, **"Aynalı Oda"** (70) (Room with Mirrors), which has never been photographed is seen. On the left of the courtyard, on a plane 6 m. below, there is a pool (62). Near it is a punishment room where, most probably, guilty maids were closed in. The complaints and verses of lament written on the walls of this room give at least a little hint about it.

The last stop of the trip is the corridor known as **"Altın Yol"** (64) (Golden Way). It is said that sultans would pass from here on special days and distribute gold to the slaves who wait for him here. On this corridor there happened an attempt of assassination to Sultan Mahmud II (1808-39), but this attempt was prevented with the help of Devriye Master (Senior Guard), who was vigilant and who helped the sultan to escape up the stairs and poured charcoals on to the pursuers.

47

EXPLANATION OF THE TERMS

Ağa : Gentleman, sir, elder brother, Feudal landlord in the Ottomans

Derviş : Somebody who begs, philosopher who makes good wishes in the name of human kind.

Hafız : Someone who knows Koran by heart.

Halife : Caliph, head of all Sunnis, representative of Mohammad.

Hamam : A room for having bath which is vaulted and paved with marble.

Hoca : Muslim clerical man, teacher, master.

Imam : Clerical man who directs the religious service at the mosque, the head of Shiites.

Kadı : Muslim judge who takes canon law as the legal basis.

Köçekçe : Male dancer who dances in women's clothes.

Kuran Kursu : A course at which children learn the arabic abc and writing.

Kurban Bayramı : A religious holiday when Muslims sacrifice rams, calves or camels and distribute their meat to poor people.

Lale Devri : Tulip Period, a period of entertainment of the Ottomans between the years of 1718 and 1730.

Medrese : High Koran course at the Ottoman Period.

Mihrab : The part of the mosques directed at Kaaba, which the muslims turn their faces towards while performing their religious service.

Minber : A part of the mosque standing on the left of mihrab, which has a sharp vault and steps going up to it, and where imam preaches.

Minare : Minaret, long and narrow sections of the mosques, which have spiral steps and one or more gallery from which the call for prayer was used to be made.

Rakkase : Female dancers.

Ramazan Bayramı : One of the five conditions that muslims have to obey, a month in which all bodily needs and pleasures are forbidden between the rise and setting of the sun.

Padişah : Soveriegn of the Ottomans, Sultan.

Paşa : A rank at military and civil service, (Excellency).

Sadrazam : The senior of viziers and people working at civil service, the most efficient servant of the sultan.

Saray : Palace, Serail.

Sazende : A group of musicians.

Şeyhülislam : The highest rank representative of Islam within the borders of the Ottoman Empire.

Sultan : The sovereign at Sunni societies, a title that the daughters, mothers and sisters of the sovereigns use after their names.

Sure : Verses in Koran

Sehzade : Son of a Sultan.

Taht : Throne

Tesbih : Beads.

Turban : Turban, scarf.

Türbe : Tomb, grave, mausoleum.

Vizir : Vizier, minister